BOOTS 179
MGS

↙ **PART ONE**
TDS

SMASH 137

MR. WANY

KING 157
RTM

DEFER
K2S

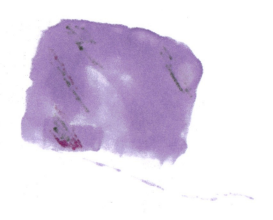

DOCK

ERM ONE
FMB

SABE
FYS

PEKOR
FB CREW

SHIRO

SCORE
BLUES

SHEAS

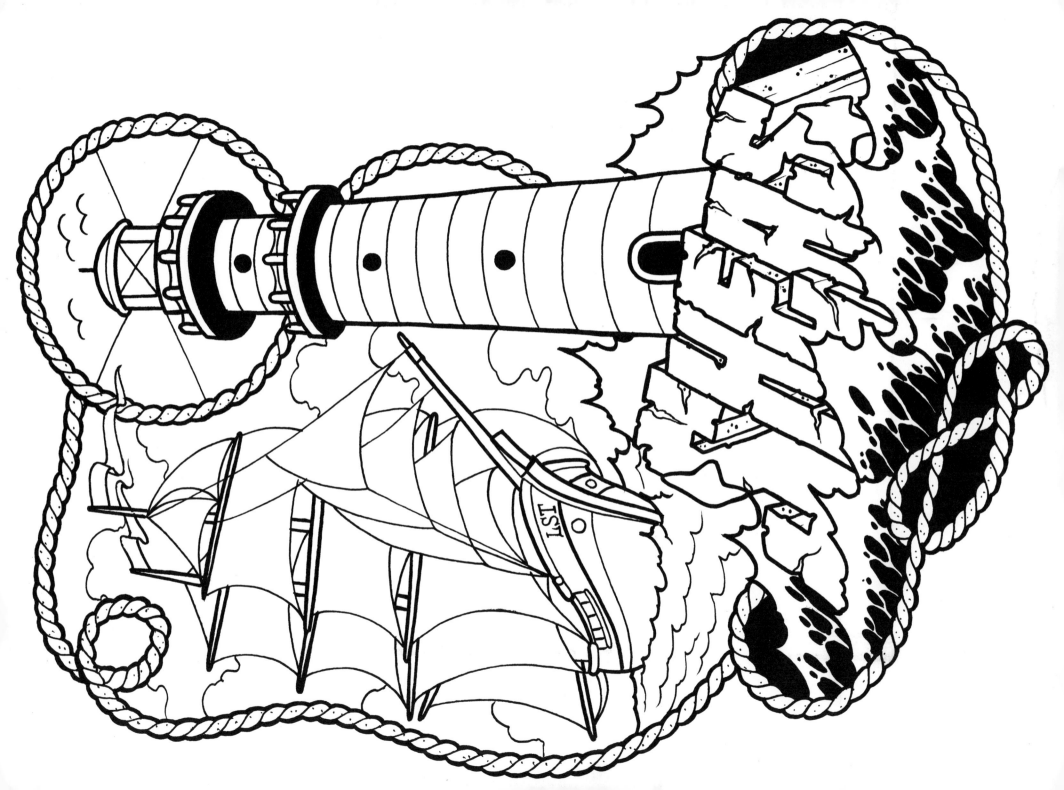

LOOMIT

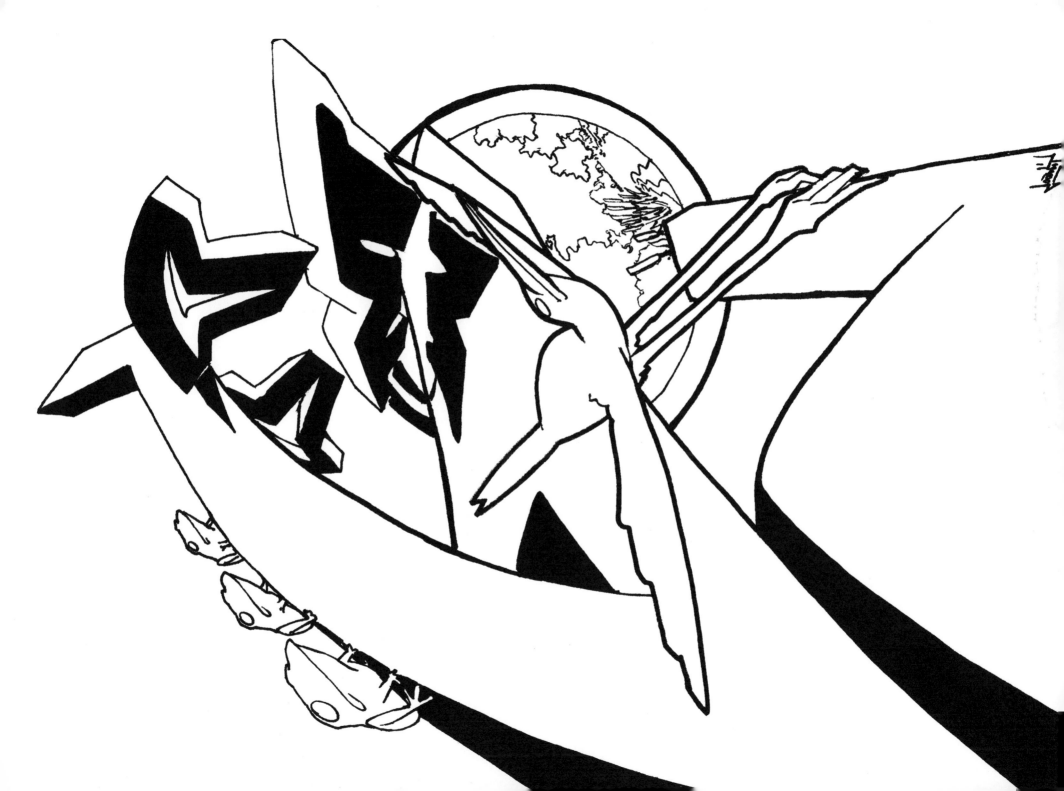

MOTEL

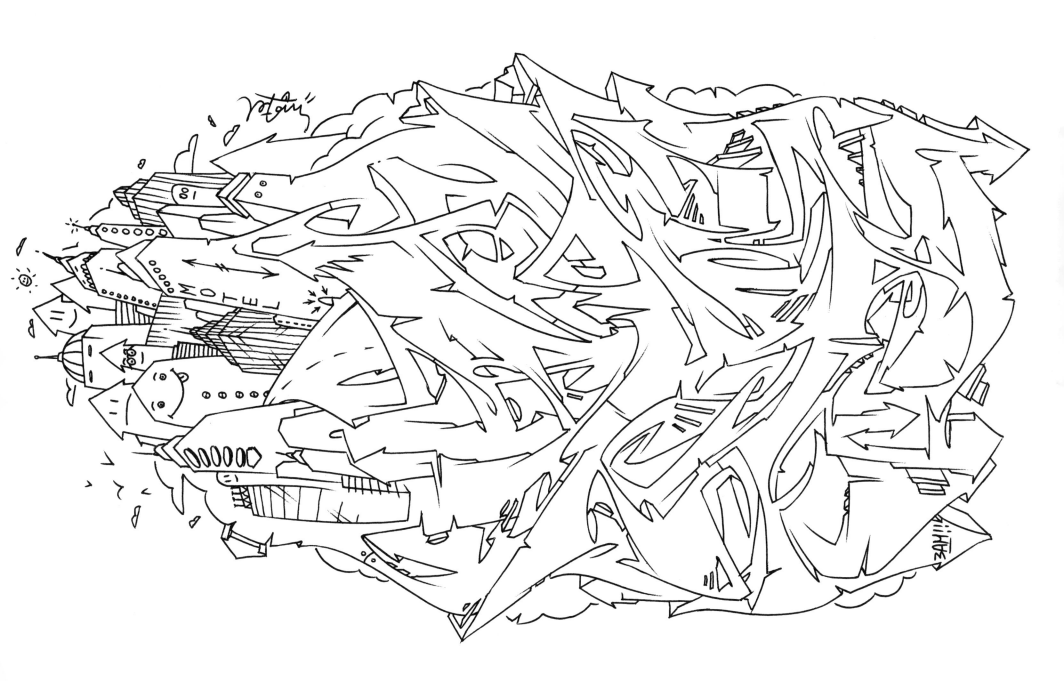

ROSKO
CAF

KLUB 7

44 FLAVOURS

DOES

CANTWO

DAIM

BINHO
3°M

JAES
COD, TNB

YES 2

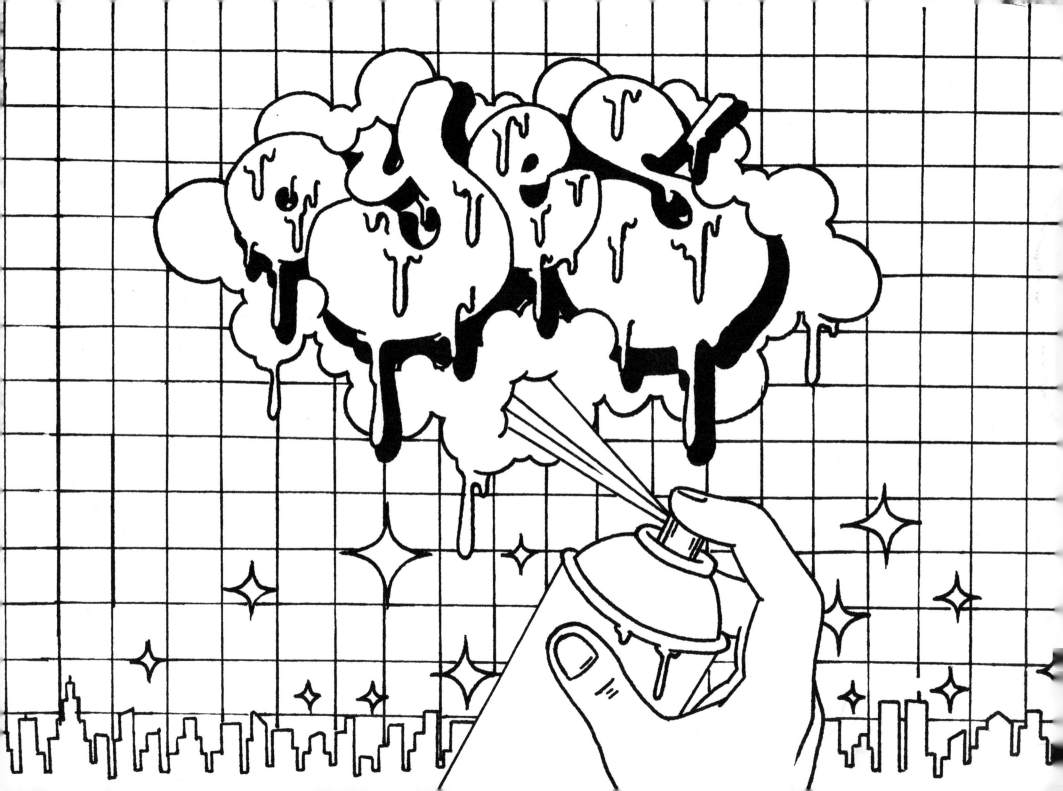

Special thanks to all participating artists!

Coverart by SHIRO
Posterart by KLUB 7

First published in 2010 by:

FROM HERE TO FAME
PUBLISHING

Marienburgerstr. 16 A
10405 Berlin/Germany
info@fhtf.de
www.fromheretofame.com

ISBN 978-3-937946-19-1 / English version
ISBN 978-3-937946-20-7 / German version

Printed and bound in China

© From Here To Fame Publishing 2010
© Art by the Artists

All rights reserved. No part of this publication may be reproduced, stored in a retrieval system or transmitted in any form or by any means, electronic or mechanical including photocopy, recording or any other information storage or retrieval system, without prior permission from the publisher.